*To the amazing BPP team: Charlie, Jenny, Olivia,
Winsome, Sarah and Russell – M.R.*

For my parents, my captains from the Lower Rhine – D.B.

BIG PICTURE PRESS

First published in the UK in 2025 by Big Picture Press,
an imprint of Bonnier Books UK,
5th Floor, HYLO, 103–105 Bunhill Row,
London, EC1Y 8LZ
Owned by Bonnier Books
Sveavägen 56, Stockholm, Sweden
www.bonnierbooks.co.uk

Text copyright © 2025 by Matt Ralphs
Illustration copyright © 2025 by Dieter Braun
Design copyright © 2025 by Big Picture Press

1 3 5 7 9 10 8 6 4 2

All rights reserved

ISBN 978-1-80078-735-3

This book was typeset in Bourton Hand, Modern Appliances, Javiera and Al kelso
The illustrations were created and coloured digitally

Edited by Joanna McInerney and Russell McLean
Art directed by Winsome d'Abreu
Production by Neil Randles

Printed in China

NAUTICAL

MATT RALPHS

DIETER BRAUN

CONTENTS

INTRODUCTION 6

ANCIENT VESSELS 8

EXTRAORDINARY VESSELS: DRAGONSHIPS 10

MEDIEVAL VESSELS 12

EXTRAORDINARY VESSELS: *MARY ROSE* 14

THE AGE OF SAIL: EXPLORATION 16

FIRST TIME AROUND THE WORLD 18

THE AGE OF SAIL: TRADE 20

EXTRAORDINARY VESSELS: *CUTTY SARK* 22

SHIPYARDS 24

CONTAINER PORTS 26

THE AGE OF SAIL: WARFARE 28

EXTRAORDINARY VESSELS: HMS *VICTORY* 30

THE GOLDEN AGE OF PIRACY 32

EXTRAORDINARY VESSELS: *WHYDAH GALLY* 34

THE AGE OF THE STEAMSHIP	36
EXTRAORDINARY VESSELS: *MONITOR* AND *VIRGINIA*	38
IMPERIAL TRANS-ANTARCTIC EXPEDITION	40
CARGO SHIPS	42
FISHING BOATS	43
EXTRAORDINARY VESSELS: RMS *TITANIC*	44
THE AGE OF THE STEEL SHIP	46
BATTLESHIPS	48
AIRCRAFT CARRIERS	50
SUBMARINES	52
EXTRAORDINARY VESSELS: *TRIESTE*	54
RESCUE BOATS AND LIFEBOATS	56
LEISURE AND RACING BOATS	57
BOATS TIMELINE	58
RECORD BREAKERS	60
GLOSSARY	62
INDEX	64

INTRODUCTION

The world we live in today has a dizzying array of vehicles. Those that travel across land, those that soar in the sky, even those that escape our planet altogether and ply the cold darkness of space. We can fly to the other side of the globe in a day, reach remote mountaintops or islands by helicopter, and traverse deserts and steppe in automobiles. And yet, not so long ago, all this was impossible.

Before the invention of the internal combustion engine in the late 19th century, all land vehicles were powered by human or animal muscle, and flying contraptions were impractical. Now, imagine going even further back in time to when the wheel was yet to be invented (around 4000 BCE). No land vehicles at all then (except, perhaps, sleds). One form of transport did exist, however, and had been around for many thousands of years. Boats.

The reason boats were invented so much earlier than land vehicles is because they don't require wheels or machinery to function. Movement is easy because water creates very little friction and allows the passage of anything that floats. The first waterborne vehicles were rafts, constructed from around 60,000 years ago by lashing buoyant logs together to form a floating platform. The first boats were hollowed-out tree trunks powered either by oars or by hand. We can only imagine the feeling of freedom that prehistoric humans first experienced when they set off from some lakeshore in a dugout boat: watching the land recede from view, sensing the water slip effortlessly past, hearing the gentle lap of the waves.

These days, waterborne vehicles come in all shapes, sizes and designs, and are an essential and integral part of our modern world. Cargo vessels haul our trade goods, passenger liners transport us from home to holiday destinations, warships protect our shores, rowboats provide leisure, speedboats excitement, and submarines explore the ocean depths.

So, put on your captain's hat, haul up the anchor and prepare to sail the high seas!

ANCIENT VESSELS

Before the invention of the internal combustion engine in the late 19th century, the fastest and most reliable way to both travel and transport cargo was not over land, but by water. For at least 10,000 years humans have used boats on lakes and rivers, and later, after the invention of oar- and sail-powered ships, on the oceans too. This advance opened up a new world of exploration, trade and conflict.

Polynesian voyaging canoes were built from around 3,000 years ago by Southeast Asian explorers during their epic voyages of discovery into the Pacific Ocean. Their two wooden hulls, lashed together with rope and boards, provided a stable platform even in heavy seas, and their sharp hulls sliced easily through the water. This design is so effective that it is still in use today.

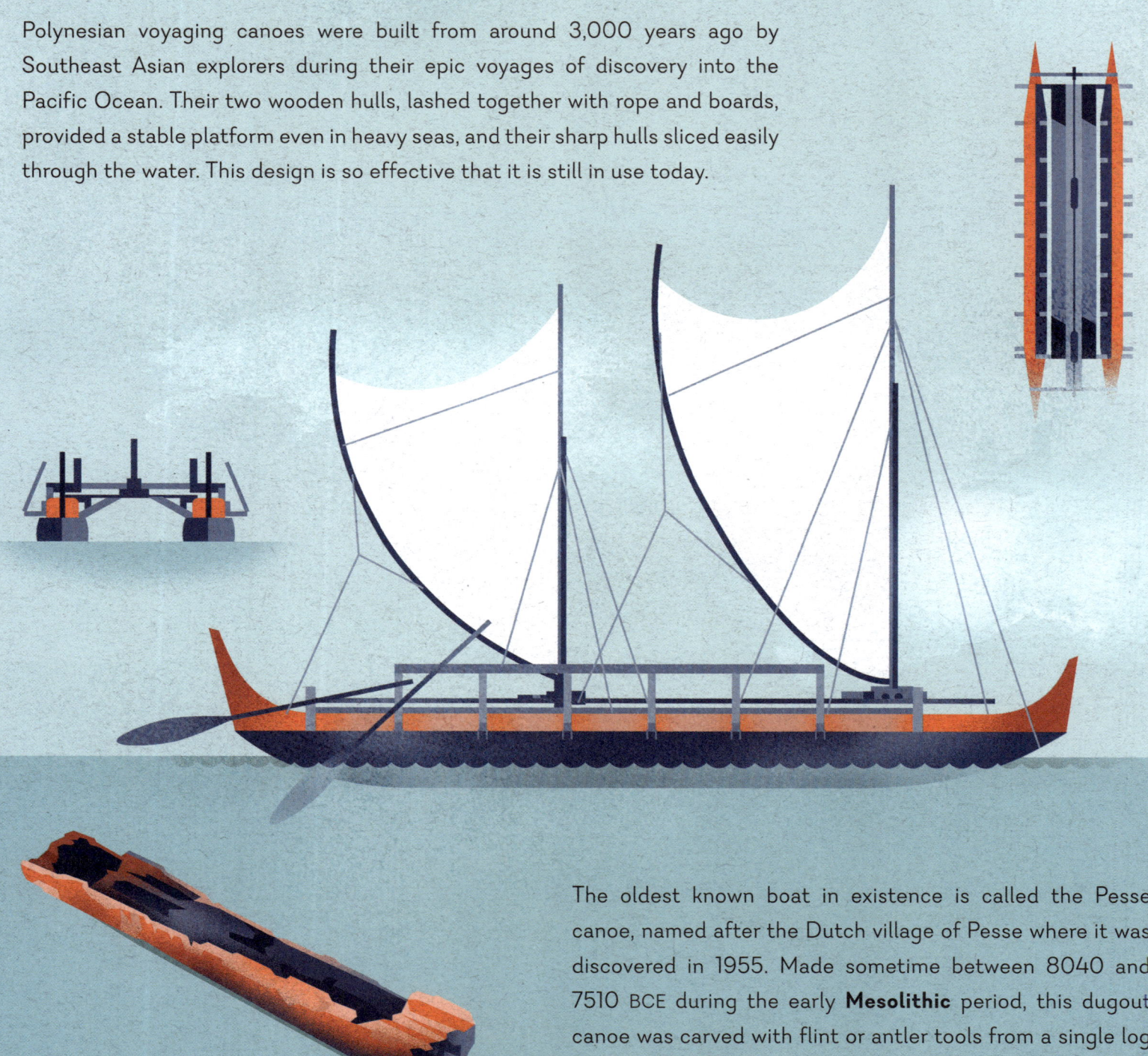

The oldest known boat in existence is called the Pesse canoe, named after the Dutch village of Pesse where it was discovered in 1955. Made sometime between 8040 and 7510 BCE during the early **Mesolithic** period, this dugout canoe was carved with flint or antler tools from a single log of a Scots pine tree. It was used by **hunter-gatherers** to travel and fish on rivers and lakes.

Constructed by the ancient Greeks from at least 800 BCE, pentecontors (meaning 'fifty-oared') were a type of galley – a long wooden vessel powered by rowers and, when the wind was favourable, a single large sail. Pentecontors were fast and highly versatile. They could carry cargo, transport soldiers, fight other vessels or carry out raids on coastal towns and villages.

Triremes were swift, manoeuvrable and powerful warships used widely by the ancient Persians, Phoenicians, Greeks and Romans during the 5th century BCE. Rowers sat in three levels below the top deck (trireme means 'three-rower' in Greek). Above them were archers to shoot at enemy vessels, and soldiers to jump onboard when they got close enough. But a trireme's most powerful weapon was the bronze ram fixed to the **prow** – capable of splitting timbers and puncturing hulls.

The ancient Phoenicians, who lived in what is now Lebanon, were masters of the sea. They were the first people to navigate the Mediterranean Sea. Phoenician traders used 'gauloi', or 'round ships'. These ships had wide hulls to carry plenty of cargo, and were often decorated with carved horse heads.

– EXTRAORDINARY VESSELS –
DRAGONSHIPS

During the early Middle Ages, few sights were as terrifying as a dragonship bearing swiftly down onto a beach: the fearsomely carved figurehead looming through the sea-mist; oars rhythmically rising and dipping; a blood-red sail fat with wind – and an eager crew, fully armed and ready to raid, steal and capture slaves.

Between 800 and 1200 CE, Vikings (people of Scandinavia, also called the Norse) ruled the seas of northern Europe. No one could match their navigational skills and state-of-the-art vessels. With their sleek oak hulls designed to slice through water like a hot knife through butter, dragonships were the most advanced boats of their time. The ship was powered through the water by a single woollen sail and two rows of oars.

Instead of benches, rowers sat on wooden chests which also held their personal belongings, while weapons and food were stashed under the deck. Although immensely strong, dragonships were lightweight enough for the crew to drag them across dry land.

Life onboard dragonships was challenging: Vikings often had to row for hours on heavy seas. Voyages could last for weeks, and there was no shelter from the wind, rain or sun. All this hardship was exhausting, but it gave the men strength and stamina – useful attributes when it was time to fight. Many historians believe it was a Viking called Leif Erikson who was the first European to cross the Atlantic and set foot on continental North America. This proves just how remarkable the Vikings and their dragonships really were.

MEDIEVAL VESSELS

Although ancient vessels (see pages 8–9) were still used throughout the medieval period (500–1500 CE), advances in technology allowed naval architects to design bigger, better and more durable ships. These vessels could travel further and carry extra cargo, allowing for more profitable trade between distant nations. European explorers could venture into the open oceans to discover new places, establishing trade routes and expanding empires – often at the expense of the indigenous people living there.

Knarrs were a type of longboat used by the Vikings for trade, transport and exploration. Like the dragonship, a knarr was sail- and oar-powered, but the hull was taller and wider to allow more cargo to be loaded. Trade items included wool, timber, wheat and furs, which were transported all over northern Europe, the Mediterranean, and Norse settlements in Iceland and Greenland.

Invented in China during the 2nd century CE, junks are large wooden ships that are still sailed today. The first junks were sail-powered and used for transport, trade and warfare whereas modern junks have engines and are used for transport and leisure trips. Their wedge-shaped prows, wide hulls, tall sides and flat bottoms allow junks to navigate shallow waters as well as the high seas.

Used across the seas of northern Europe, cogs were sturdy and reliable cargo vessels, capable of carrying much more than the smaller knarr. Powered by a single **square sail** and steered with a rudder, cogs were more manoeuvrable than their tubby shape made them appear, and they could navigate the open sea as well as traverse wide rivers to reach inland ports.

Galleys were sailed widely in ancient times and remained popular in the medieval period, especially with the great Mediterranean powers of the Venetian republic, and the Byzantine and Ottoman empires. Armed galleys were favoured by pirates, who ventured out from their bases on the North African coast to attack ships and raid coastal villages.

Caravels were swift, nimble and capable of ocean voyages and navigating shallow coastlines, coves and rivers – making them the perfect choice for trading, exploring and fighting. Powered by either square or **lateen sails** (sometimes both) and armed with cannons, these versatile vessels were widely utilised, especially by European nations.

– EXTRAORDINARY VESSELS –
MARY ROSE

On 19 July 1545 England faced an invasion. Francis I, King of France, had assembled an **armada** of around 200 vessels – sailing ships and oared galleys – and sent it across the narrow English Channel to offload a French army of 30,000 men on the south coast. England's King Henry VIII's far smaller fleet, of around 80 vessels, would need to prevent the armada from landing. As evening fell, and taking advantage of a fresh rising breeze, the English sailed out to meet their enemy. At the head, **pennants** fluttering and bristling with around 70 guns, sped the mighty 800-tonne carrack warship *Mary Rose*, pride of the fleet and King Henry's favourite vessel.

Smoke and flame erupted along *Mary Rose*'s **port** side as its cannons fired at the approaching French ships.

To the thousands of people watching from the cliffs, the noise would have sounded like thunder. Then, to bring its **starboard** guns into the action as the others were reloaded, the grand old ship began to turn about... and at that crucial moment a gust of wind hit its sails, causing it to **list**. Water poured in through the still-open gunports, flooding the lower decks.

Realising their ship was doomed, the sailors and soldiers scrambled to reach the open **weather deck** and leap overboard, only to be trapped by the **anti-boarding netting** strung over it. Seawater foamed around them, rising higher and higher... From his vantage point on Southsea Castle, King Henry himself watched the *Mary Rose* capsize and disappear beneath the waves. Of around 400 men onboard, only 35 escaped with their lives.

THE AGE OF SAIL: EXPLORATION

Imagine setting out into an unexplored ocean in a small wooden sailing ship with no idea what dangers await over the horizon. Storms or shallow reefs could wreck the vessel, starvation and disease could kill the crew, or an unpopular or unlucky captain could face **mutiny**. And yet, lured by the possibility of fame and untold wealth, many European explorers did just that during the 15th to 17th centuries, a period called the Age of Exploration.

Long-distance exploration required vessels capable of withstanding bad weather and heavy seas, and with holds big enough to carry the food, water and equipment for the voyage (with room to spare for any cargo picked up on the way). The carrack, developed in Portugal and Spain during the 14th century, met these requirements. Equipped with three (sometimes four) masts, a roomy hold and capable of carrying cannons, these versatile vessels sailed from Europe all over the globe on missions of discovery, trade and conquest.

The Age of Exploration affected the world in many ways. The further exploration of known continents like Africa and the discovery of unknown ones such as the Americas, increased Europe's knowledge of the world's geography and ocean currents. It also created contact with many other societies, cultures and nations. The resulting trade in luxury goods such as spices, sugar, tobacco and precious metals created huge wealth, especially for Spain, Portugal, the Netherlands and Great Britain.

No matter how much money these nations made, however, it was never enough. And so began a ruthless rush among Europe's most powerful countries to conquer, subdue and exploit the indigenous people they encountered – especially in Africa and the Americas – and steal their natural resources, often with great cruelty and violence.

Europeans brought death not only by sword and musket, but also by introducing diseases such as smallpox and typhus, to which the indigenous people had no natural resistance. Millions died. On top of this human tragedy, millions more were enslaved: displaced from their homes and forced to work down mines or on plantations in terrible conditions.

FIRST TIME AROUND THE WORLD

In 1518, Portuguese sailor Ferdinand Magellan made an offer to King Charles I of Spain. In return for funding and a fleet of ships, he would seek out and discover a western trade route to the Spice Islands, located on the other side of the world. Success would allow the import of expensive luxuries such as nutmeg and cloves – and bring untold riches to Spain. The king agreed, and so began one of the most incredible sea voyages ever attempted.

1) In September 1519, Magellan set sail from Spain with 270 men in five carrack sailing ships – the *Trinidad*, *San Antonio*, *Santiago*, *Concepción* and *Victoria* – and supplies for two years.

2) Magellan's fleet battled through terrifying storms, lashing winds and heavy seas on their journey southwards along the West African coast.

3) After surviving the months-long Atlantic crossing and a mutiny by the captain of the *San Antonio*, Magellan was relieved to reach South America unscathed. Ships were repaired and supplies of food and water replenished.

4) The fleet sailed south, looking for a passage through South America that would lead them to the ocean beyond… and the Spice Islands. The *Santiago* was wrecked during a fierce storm, but the crew were rescued.

9) Three years after sailing out and having circumnavigated the globe for the first time in history, Elcano arrived back in Spain in September 1522. Only 18 of his men remained alive, but their places in history were assured.

8) Command fell to Spanish navigator Juan Sebastián Elcano, who led the depleted fleet to the Spice Islands. They had made it! . Elcano filled the *Victoria*'s hold with spices and set off home, leaving the damaged and leaking *Trinidad* behind.

7) When the fleet reached the Philippines in March 1521, Magellan set about trying to convert the indigenous islanders to Christianity. Some agreed – but others resisted, and on 27 April, Magellan was killed by warriors on Mactan Island while landing with an armed force.

6) With no idea how vast the Pacific was, Magellan and his men didn't see land again for over three months. Starvation and disease ravaged the crew, who had to survive on rancid water, rotten biscuits and even leather. Around 20 men died.

5) Magellan found the sea passage (later named the Strait of Magellan) to the Sea of the South (which he renamed the Pacific) on 21 October 1520. There was still unrest among the fleet, however, and the *San Antonio*'s crew deserted and headed back to Spain.

THE AGE OF SAIL: TRADE

During the Golden Age of Sail (late 15th to mid-19th century), European explorers navigated to new lands, took note of any valuable natural resources (such as tea, coffee, sugar and cocoa) and sailed home to report their findings. The most powerful European nations – including Britain, Spain, Portugal, France and the Netherlands – were eager to secure these lands and commodities for themselves. Centuries of invasion and occupation followed. Natural resources and cultural artefacts were plundered, and millions of indigenous people were ruthlessly exploited, transported and enslaved.

The many types of merchant sailing ships that transported the bulk of overseas trade between the 16th and 19th centuries were known collectively as East Indiamen. They were generally large, with roomy holds, and built to be sturdy (although later designs such as the Blackwall frigate and tea clipper (see page 22) were built for speed). As well as being big, they were also armed with cannons to protect themselves and their precious cargo from **marauding** pirates.

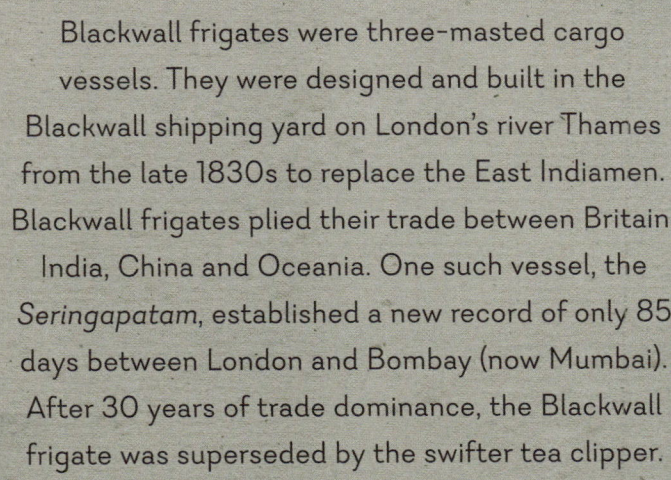

Blackwall frigates were three-masted cargo vessels. They were designed and built in the Blackwall shipping yard on London's river Thames from the late 1830s to replace the East Indiamen. Blackwall frigates plied their trade between Britain, India, China and Oceania. One such vessel, the *Seringapatam*, established a new record of only 85 days between London and Bombay (now Mumbai). After 30 years of trade dominance, the Blackwall frigate was superseded by the swifter tea clipper.

It's estimated that around 12 million Africans were forced into slavery by European powers between the 16th and 19th centuries. Torn from their homes, they endured the long Atlantic crossings to plantations in the Caribbean and Americas onboard specially designed slave ships. To maximise profits, ship owners packed in as many enslaved people as possible. This led to unbearably hot and cramped conditions below deck, where oxygen was sometimes so low that candles couldn't burn. Disease, dehydration, exhaustion and mistreatment killed many.

– EXTRAORDINARY VESSELS –
CUTTY SARK

There must have been no finer sight in the mid-19th century than *Cutty Sark* in full sail, its sleek hull heeling hard over in the wind and racing across the sea. *Cutty Sark* (now exhibited in Greenwich, London) is a clipper – a type of ship designed entirely for speed. Its task was to bring precious trade commodities such as tea from faraway China to Britain's ports faster than its rivals. Clippers such as the *Thermopylae*, *Fiery Cross* and *Ariel* were well-known to people at the time, and their progress was followed with great interest in the newspapers.

Clippers were a world away from the more ordinary, heavy, wide-hulled cargo vessels also used at that time. *Cutty Sark* has what is known as a 'composite hull', which is a wooden hull built around an iron frame. This made the ship

strong and rigid enough to survive long ocean voyages, and lightweight enough to sail swiftly. Clipper hulls were also narrow, which meant they couldn't carry as large a load as earlier cargo ships but, powered by a large expanse of sail hanging from three masts, they travelled around three times faster. Competitive captains often kept all sails raised even during storms, trusting the timbers to take the strain and see them safely – and swiftly – home.

Captains reported that *Cutty Sark* hardly disturbed the water, even when racing along at a top speed of around 16 **knots** (30 km/h). For ten years, it held the speed record between Australia and England, covering the distance in only 73 days, once travelling 672 km in only 24 hours. Despite its size (65 metres long, 11 metres wide, and with a 47-metre-tall main mast) *Cutty Sark* only needed a crew of around 26 people.

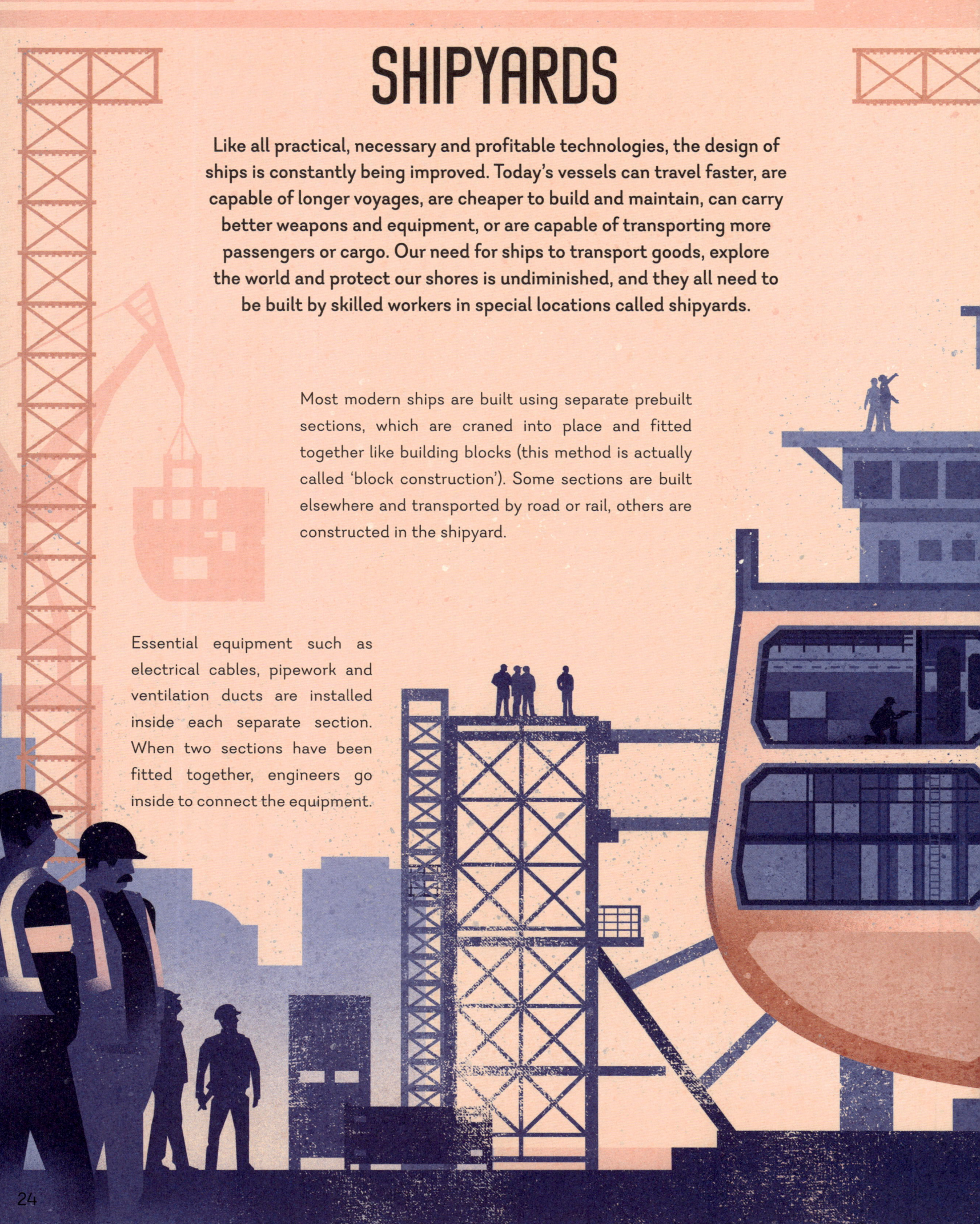

SHIPYARDS

Like all practical, necessary and profitable technologies, the design of ships is constantly being improved. Today's vessels can travel faster, are capable of longer voyages, are cheaper to build and maintain, can carry better weapons and equipment, or are capable of transporting more passengers or cargo. Our need for ships to transport goods, explore the world and protect our shores is undiminished, and they all need to be built by skilled workers in special locations called shipyards.

Most modern ships are built using separate prebuilt sections, which are craned into place and fitted together like building blocks (this method is actually called 'block construction'). Some sections are built elsewhere and transported by road or rail, others are constructed in the shipyard.

Essential equipment such as electrical cables, pipework and ventilation ducts are installed inside each separate section. When two sections have been fitted together, engineers go inside to connect the equipment.

Shipyards are equipped with various types of cranes. The largest – those used to move the ship sections into place and hold them while they are being connected – can lift hundreds of tonnes. They usually run on tracks on either side of a ship, and move components up, down and horizontally. Smaller fixed cranes are used to lift lighter loads. Mobile cranes run on wheels under their own power, and can be placed wherever they are needed.

Large, modern vessels are usually constructed, maintained and repaired in a dry dock. When the dock is flooded, ships can sail through the open gates. Then the gates are closed, the water in the dock is pumped out, the ship comes to rest on a dry platform and work can begin. Some ships are constructed on a slipway above the waterline and then launched down the slipway – this is often a very dramatic sight that can draw many spectators.

CONTAINER PORTS

Our world today is global, and around 90 per cent of traded goods are transported by ship. Many everyday items, from TVs to t-shirts and books to bananas, have made their way to you from another part of the world, in a box stacked up on a container ship. A whole chain of complicated events, involving several methods of transport and lots of people, will have made it possible for these products to reach you. They may have travelled thousands of kilometres across land and sea to get to your front door.

Goods are packed into containers at the factories where they are made or at the warehouses where they are stored until purchased. Once packed, the containers are loaded onto trucks or freight trains, which then transport them via road or rail to the container port. A standard 6-metre-long, 2.3-metre-wide and 2.3-metre-tall container can hold 400 flat-screen TVs or 48,000 bananas!

When the land journey is complete, the containers are taken from the trucks and trains and piled up in stacks in the port's storage yard. Each container has its own unique number stamped on the outside so it can be tracked wherever it goes.

Containers are moved around the port using reach stackers, which function in a similar way to forklift trucks, and huge gantry cranes that travel on wheels or tracks. Containers are designed to be transported by truck, train and ship without needing to be unpacked when transferring between them. This makes their journey as fast and efficient as possible.

When the ship is ready, all the containers are loaded on board. Correct placement is important: containers due to be unloaded at the first port of call are stacked at the top; those due at the final port are stacked at the bottom. Incredibly, there are around 20 million containers being carried on the high seas at any one time.

The biggest container ships can carry over 24,000 containers. When all the containers are safely secured, the ship begins its voyage, stopping off at various ports and offloading the correct containers. They are then moved, stored and transferred to trucks and trains to be taken to their final destinations.

THE AGE OF SAIL: WARFARE

On land, battles are fought with armies. On sea, they're fought with navies. During the Age of Sail, the most powerful European nations built grand fleets of warships at great cost. They were used to defend ports, trade routes and trade shipping from pirates and hostile nations. Warships were also used to attack enemy ships, assist in land invasions and, to inflict financial hardship, blockade harbours to prevent the flow of goods. Navies were essential – without them, these empires would have crumbled.

From the 17th century, carracks and galleons were replaced by 'ships of the line' – a type of sailing warship. By the end of the 18th century, these ships of the line came in three sizes: first-rates were the largest, with over 100 guns on three decks; second-rates had up to 100 guns on three decks; and third-rates up to 80 guns on two decks. Fleets used 'line of battle' tactics. **Admirals** lined up their fleets in single file and, when level with the enemy, let loose devastating close-range volleys of cannon fire called broadsides. The victor was usually the side that maintained a superior rate of fire.

Battles during the Age of Sail were noisy, chaotic and frightening. Upon spotting the enemy, the whole crew leapt into action. The captain and officers gathered on deck to give their orders, and coloured flags were used to pass messages and instructions to the rest of the fleet. Marines with muskets climbed up the masts to their sharpshooting positions. Sand was spread on deck to stop men from slipping. The surgeon laid out his tools, ready to receive the wounded, and the galley stove was extinguished to reduce fire risk. Carpenters made ready to plug holes shot beneath the waterline, and sailors operated pumps to get rid of any seawater leaking inside.

During a ship of the line battle, around three quarters of the crew were needed to operate the cannons. It was heavy, exhausting, dangerous work, and the cramped gun decks quickly filled with smoke, flying splinters and the cries of the wounded. Solid round-shot was used to puncture hulls – not to sink a ship, but rather cause chaos, injury and death to the enemy crew. Chain-shot and bar-shot split masts and ripped through rigging. Canister-shot and grapeshot turned cannons into deadly giant shotguns.

– EXTRAORDINARY VESSELS –
HMS VICTORY

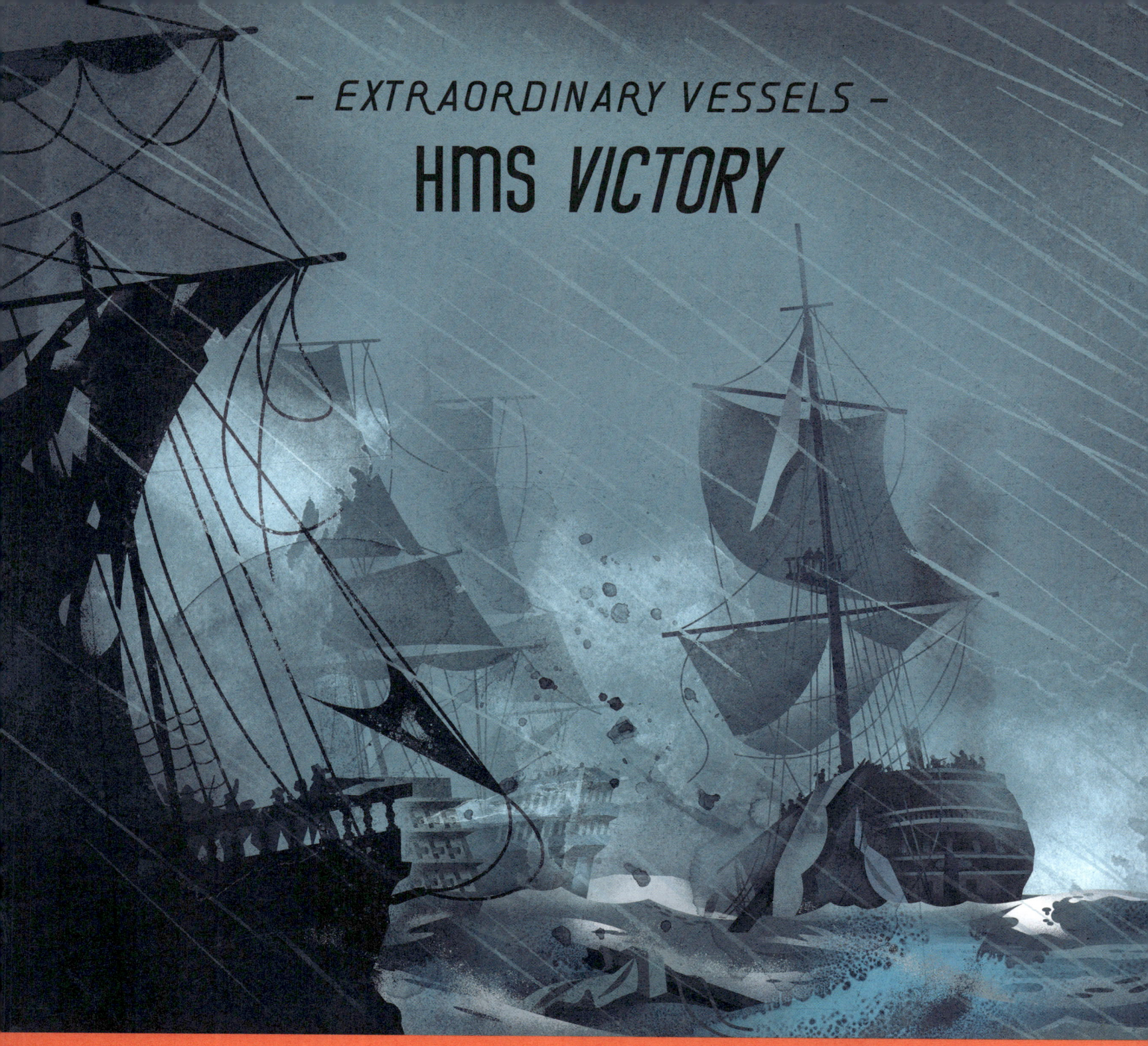

Launched in 1765, with a crew of around 850 men and 104 cannons, British Royal Navy first-rate ship of the line HMS *Victory* was one of the most powerful warships of its era. Two thousand oak trees were cut and carved to make the hull, it had 37 sails and, with a top speed of around 10 knots (18.5 km/h), was faster than most ships its size. HMS *Victory* fought in several important battles, but is most famous as the flagship of Vice Admiral Horatio Nelson during his crushing victory over the French and Spanish in the Battle of Trafalgar in 1805.

HMS *Victory* had a skilled and disciplined crew where every man knew his role. The captain was in charge, assisted by 13 officers. There were 21 midshipmen – officer cadets, some as young as 13, serving six-year apprenticeships.

Eight warrant officers held specialist jobs, including navigator, surgeon, chaplain, carpenter (in charge of repairs), gunner (responsible for the cannons), and boatswain (pronounced 'bo-sun', in charge of sails and rigging). One hundred and thirteen clerks, stewards, petty officers and mates assisted the officers.

There were also 492 sailors split into three ranks ('able', 'ordinary' and 'landsmen'), who (among many other things) raised and lowered sails and anchors, scrubbed the deck and, during battle, manned the cannons. Thirty-one ship's boys did various jobs such as assisting the cook or surgeon, and general fetching and carrying; they were often orphans or destitutes who joined the Royal Navy on the promise of food and shelter. A complement of 142 marines – soldiers at sea – maintained discipline on ship and fought during battles.

THE GOLDEN AGE OF PIRACY

Between 1650 and 1730, in the trade-rich waters of the Atlantic, Caribbean Sea and Indian Ocean, pirates reigned supreme. Rogue captains and crews of many nationalities prowled the seas in search of prey. No one was safe from these pistol- and cutlass-wielding thieves: fishing and merchant ships were raided for their cargo and, on the rarest occasions, galleons were attacked for their gold. Pirates even formed an alliance called the Pirate Republic, which operated from a base on the island of New Providence in the Bahamas.

Bristol-born Edward 'Blackbeard' Teach is the most infamous of the Golden Age pirates. Commanding his 40-gun ship *Queen Anne's Revenge* in the Caribbean, Blackbeard adopted a deliberately terrifying appearance to intimidate his victims into surrendering without a fight. He met his end during a ferocious battle on the deck of his ship; it took five pistol shots and twenty sword strikes to kill him.

John 'Calico Jack' Rackham had a short but eventful pirate career in the Caribbean between 1718 and 1720. His crew included two fearsome women, Anne Bonny and Mary Read. Rackham and his crew were eventually captured after a battle with a pirate hunter. Rackham was hanged for his crimes; Bonny and Read claimed to be pregnant so were spared execution and imprisoned.

Starting his life at sea at 13 years old, Bartholomew 'Black Bart' Roberts soon realised there was money to be made as a pirate. Backed by a loyal crew, Roberts went on to become the most successful pirate of the Golden Age, plundering around 450 vessels in only three years. He was killed in 1722 by cannon fire from a Royal Navy warship off the west coast of Africa.

Captain of the 30-gun **sloop** *Ranger* and leader of a pirate fleet, Benjamin Hornigold plundered the shipping lanes of the Caribbean. He helped establish the Pirate Republic, was known to be kind to his prisoners, and had Edward 'Blackbeard' Teach among his crew. After being pardoned for his crimes, Hornigold turned pirate-hunter, but was killed when his ship was wrecked during a hurricane in 1719.

– EXTRAORDINARY VESSELS –
WHYDAH GALLY

It's 1717 in the Caribbean Sea. A British cargo ship, the 300-tonne, three-masted *Whydah Gally*, its hold packed with gold, ivory and indigo dye, has been chased for three days by a brace of pirate ships. With a boom and a plume of smoke, one of the pursuing sloops fires off a shot; realising the game is up, the captain of the *Whydah Gally* lowers his flag and surrenders. He's lucky. The pirate captain is Samuel Bellamy, famous for showing mercy to the crews he captures. Bellamy – a dashing figure with a long velvet coat, silver-buckled shoes and four pistols tucked into a sash – takes the *Whydah Gally* as his new flagship, adds more cannons, and sails up the east American coast seeking more prizes.

Devon-born Bellamy – nicknamed the Prince of Pirates – only operated for about a year. But in that short time, it's believed he plundered at least 54 vessels and stole enough treasure to make him the richest pirate

of the Golden Age. He commanded two vessels – the powerful 28-gun *Whydah Gally* (Bellamy added more firepower when he took over the vessel) and a smaller, faster sloop – and possessed an expert grasp of naval tactics, ensuring that most victims surrendered to Bellamy without firing a shot. But, as with all pirates, death was always close, and in 1717 the *Whydah Gally* and her sister ship were caught in a storm and sunk off the coast of Cape Cod, taking their vast treasure hoards down with them. Bellamy and most of his crew drowned.

But the *Whydah Gally*'s story did not end on that fateful night, because in 1984 the wreck was discovered buried under the seabed. Many artefacts have been recovered, including gold bars, silver and gold coins, jewellery, the ship's bell (inscribed 'The *Whydah Gally* 1716'), **swivel guns** and cannons, tools and gaming pieces. Divers also found an ornate pistol, still equipped with a red silk sash that might, perhaps, have belonged to the Prince of Pirates himself.

THE AGE OF THE STEAM SHIP

The invention of the steam engine in the late 17th century and its continued development led to a transport revolution. On land, steam locomotives clattered swiftly along steel rails. At sea, steamships carried people and cargo all over the world. Using engines fed with coal (and later, oil), steamships didn't need the wind, and so could travel anywhere at a consistent speed. This allowed people and cargo to be transported worldwide safely, regularly and efficiently.

SS *Archimedes* (SS stands for 'steamship') was the first vessel to be successfully powered by a steam-driven screw propeller, when it was launched in 1838. Screw propellers, located below the waterline and at the stern of a ship, are more efficient and reliable than paddlewheels.

Launched in 1840, RMS *Britannia* was one of the first ocean-going steamships (RMS stands for 'Royal Mail Ship') and could carry 115 passengers plus crew. A coal-fired engine turned two large paddlewheels, which powered the vessel through the water. However, RMS *Britannia* also had three masts, meaning it could make speed using the wind.

Designed by famous engineer Isambard Kingdom Brunel, SS *Great Britain* was by far the largest passenger ship of the mid-19th century. With an iron hull and powered by sails and a screw propeller (Brunel was greatly influenced by the SS *Archimedes*), it was built to carry 360 passengers across the Atlantic. SS *Great Britain* is now preserved as a museum ship in Bristol, UK.

After witnessing the success of SS *Archimedes*, the British Royal Navy launched HMS *Rattler* in 1843. Armed with nine guns, it was one of the first screw propeller warships. Along with paddlewheel warships such as HMS *Cyclops* and USS *Missouri*, HMS *Rattler* showed that the age of sail-powered warships was drawing to a rapid close.

SS *Great Eastern* was a true giant of its day, designed by Brunel to carry up to 4,000 passengers non-stop between Britain and Australia. Launched in 1858, this 211-metre iron behemoth was powered by sail, the largest set of paddlewheels at that time, and a screw propeller. Brunel died aged 53 only a few days after SS *Great Eastern*'s first **sea trial**.

Just like RMS *Titanic* that launched 41 years later, SS *Oceanic* was built by Harland & Wolff and owned by the White Star Line shipping company. And, like *Titanic*, she was a beautiful ocean liner with an emphasis on comfort and luxury. Passengers enjoyed running water in their cabins, quality furniture and portholes to gaze out at the sea.

– EXTRAORDINARY VESSELS –
MONITOR AND VIRGINIA

USS *Monitor*

On 9 March 1862, during the American Civil War (1861–65), two strange vessels met in brutal combat off the coast of Virginia – and changed the course of naval warfare forever. The soldiers manning the nearby coastal forts and the sailors on their conventional wooden warships had never seen the likes of the USS *Monitor* and CSS *Virginia* before. As cannons boomed, fire blazed and smoke filled the bay, they all waited with bated breath to see which of these extraordinary duelling vessels would win the day.

Although both ships were ironclads (metal-armoured steamships), they had radically different designs. With a hull that rose only around 50 cm from the water, the USS *Monitor* looked more like a submarine than a surface ship, and was designed to be difficult to hit. Its two-gun turret could (slowly) turn 360 degrees, giving the sailors the advantage of being able to shoot in any direction regardless of where the vessel was facing.

CSS *Virginia*

CSS *Virginia* was constructed over the hull of a wooden steam frigate called the *Merrimack*. An angled wood and metal **casemate**, designed to deflect cannon balls, was built over the gun deck. It had room for 14 cannons of varying sizes, plus a ram at the front.

Both *Monitor* and *Virginia* were heavy, slow and hampered by a lack of preparation and combat practice. They circled each other, firing over and over. Cannonballs ricocheted, iron plates dented, water foamed… The heat and noise – especially inside the cramped confines of the *Monitor*'s turret – were almost unbearable. After several punishing hours, *Monitor* and *Virginia* – both wounded but still afloat – withdrew from the battle. In the end, history's first combat between ironclads was a draw. The world had seen that the age of the wooden warship was over: the future was iron.

IMPERIAL TRANS-ANTARCTIC EXPEDITION

In August 1914, sailor and polar explorer Ernest Shackleton left Portsmouth, UK, as leader of the Imperial Trans-Antarctic Expedition. His goal: to make the first land crossing of the Antarctic, via the South Pole. His ship: *Endurance*, a three-mast **barquentine** with a reinforced hull to help it force passage through the ice. After a month of preparation on South Georgia island, Shackleton and his 27-strong crew set sail and headed south...

1) Two days later, *Endurance* reached the pack ice. For several weeks the crew strove to keep the ship moving, hacking at the ice to create a path. On 18 January 1915, however, the floes pressed close and trapped the vessel. Forced to wait out the dark winter, and drifting ever-northwards on the currents, the crew settled into a routine of ship upkeep, scientific experimentation, reading and playing games.

——— *Endurance*
······· Lifeboats
- - - *Yelcho*

2) The merciless ice tightened its grip. Strong as the vessel was, *Endurance* slowly began to break up. Beams splintered, letting in water, and Shackleton ordered his men to abandon ship. They set up camp on the ice, listening to their vessel's death throes. Eventually, on 21 November, *Endurance* sank. The expedition was over. The goal now was to survive and escape the ice.

3) The crew made a home on the drifting ice floe, hoping it would take them closer to land. In April 1916, the floe began to break up; the men took to the three lifeboats and headed to Elephant Island. After a difficult five-day voyage, they landed on solid ground for the first time in 497 days.

7) His first three attempts were thwarted by thick pack ice. But, using a powerful sea **tug** called *Yelcho*, he reached Elephant Island and rescued his crew on 30 August 1916. Incredibly, after all their hardships, not a single man died during the expedition.

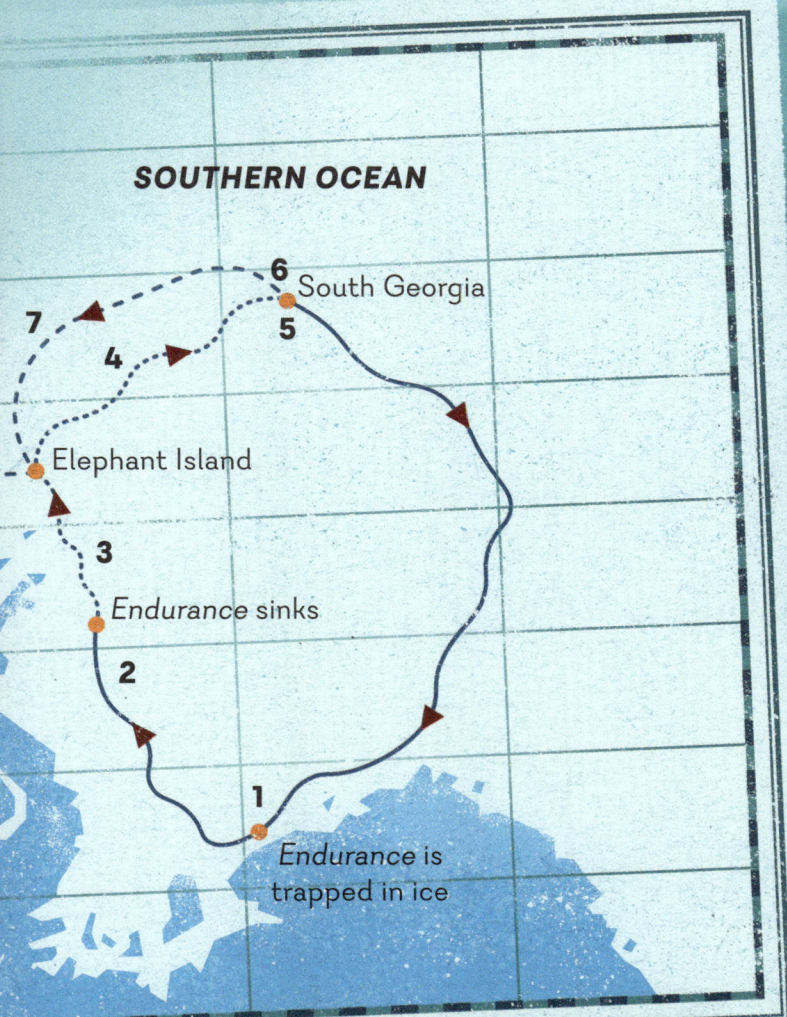

6) To reach the north coast, Shackleton led two of his men non-stop for 36 hours over glaciers and mountainous terrain with no map and no climbing gear. Exhausted and looking like scarecrows, they reached the safety of Stromness whaling station. Then, after rescuing his men on the south coast, Shackleton set his mind to those he had left behind on Elephant Island.

5) The little lifeboat was tossed like a cork on towering seas. The men bailed water dumped in by the waves and chipped ice from the masts and sails to keep their vessel from capsizing. Sleeping, cooking and navigating were almost impossible in such nightmarish conditions, yet somehow, after 16 gruelling days, they reached the south coast of South Georgia.

4) Elephant Island was remote, uninhabited and inhospitable. Using the upturned boats as shelters, the men survived on dwindling food supplies, plus the penguins and seals they hunted. Battered by fierce winds and freezing rain, the men's health and morale worsened. Shackleton had to act. With five companions, he set off in a lifeboat for South Georgia – 1,300 km away – to get help.

CARGO SHIPS

Ships are the most efficient way to transport cargo. Waterborne vehicles can be built much bigger and carry far more in their holds than trucks, trains and aeroplanes. And, of course, they can cross seas to deliver their cargo anywhere in the world. Modern cargo vessels are enormous – and yet despite their size they usually have a crew of no more than around 30 people.

There are two types of tanker. Crude tankers carry crude oil from drilling sites to refineries, and product tankers transport the refined oil products (such as petrol or diesel) to ports close to where it will be sold. Supertankers or 'ultra large crude carriers' (ULCC) are the largest mobile human-made structures in the world. The longest was the *Seawise Giant*, which stretched for nearly half a kilometre.

Container ships carry around 90 per cent of the world's seaborne cargo. They have straight sides and wide decks to fit as many containers on board as possible. These 'intermodal' containers, or shipping crates, are made from strong, rust-resistant steel and are all the same size, allowing them to be stacked together like building blocks.

Bulk carriers transport dry cargo such as cement, coal, metal ore and cereals like oats, wheat or rice. At port, the bulk cargo is loaded or poured into the hold. This must be done carefully to ensure the ship's balance is maintained – too much weight on one side can cause a vessel to capsize. Once safely loaded, hatches in the deck are sealed to keep the cargo dry and secure.

FISHING BOATS

Fishing boats are used to harvest the sea of its rich stocks of food – mostly popular fish such as tuna and cod.

Fishing trawlers drag nets known as trawls behind them as they move. The trapped fish are hauled on board, stored in giant fridges or freezers then taken back to port to be processed and sold. Modern trawlers use electronic equipment such as **GPS** navigation, **autopilots** and devices to detect shoals of fish.

Many fishing trawlers use a technique called bottom trawling. This method involves dragging a large cone-shaped net just above the seabed. These nets are designed to catch bottom-dwelling fish such as whiting, flounder, red hake, and crustaceans such as shrimp and crab. To keep the net mouth open, floats are attached to the top and weights to the bottom. When full, the net is hauled back up to the trawler.

– EXTRAORDINARY VESSELS –
RMS TITANIC

On 10 April 1912, the majestic vessel RMS *Titanic* slipped her moorings from Southampton dock and began her maiden voyage (via France and Ireland) across the Atlantic to New York. She was brand new, deemed to be practically unsinkable and, with nine decks and sixteen watertight compartments, was at the time the largest vessel afloat. It's doubtful that any of the crew or passengers would have conceived of the disaster that would befall them on a calm but cold night in four days' time.

Titanic is perhaps the most famous ship in history. Constructed by shipbuilders Harland & Wolff and owned and operated by the White Star Line, it was designed to be the most luxurious passenger liner in the world. First-class passengers paid high prices for lounges and dining rooms with the finest fixtures and fittings, amenities such as saunas, steam rooms, a swimming pool and gyms, and roomy suites with private bathrooms.

Around 70 restaurant staff – including cooks, butchers and bakers – worked around the clock to prepare thousands of meals every day, including baked salmon, steak, lobster, roast duck, puddings and ice cream.

At 11.40pm on 14 April, lookouts spotted an iceberg dead ahead. Their warning came too late and, travelling too quickly to turn in time, *Titanic*'s hull scraped against the ice. Water rushed into five of the watertight compartments, forcing the **bow** down. From that moment, the vessel was doomed. Women and children were the first to be loaded into the lifeboats (many of which were sent away barely half full), while *Titanic*'s stern rose ever upwards, exposing the enormous, now stationary propellers. Finally, around two and a half hours after striking the iceberg, *Titanic* slipped beneath the waves and sank 3,800 metres to the bottom of the sea. Of the 2,208 people on board, only around 706 survived.

THE AGE OF THE STEEL SHIP

The invention of the ironclad (see page 38) and the development of more powerful naval guns signalled the end for wooden sailing warships. From the 1860s, ship designers turned their skills to creating armoured fighting ships capable of long ocean voyages. Progress was so swift that new designs were often already obsolete before they had even launched. As the 19th century drew to a close, the biggest naval powers (led by Germany and Great Britain) were engaged in an eye-wateringly expensive, breakneck-speed race to build the biggest and best fleet of steel warships.

HMS *Dreadnought* was a particular type of battleship (see pages 48–49). Launched in 1906, its design was so influential the name 'dreadnought' was given to the entire generation of large warships that followed in its wake. Designed for long-range voyages and sea battles, dreadnoughts were powered by **steam turbine** engines and armed with around 12 large naval guns in rotating turrets.

Battlecruisers were large **capital ships**. They had smaller guns than dreadnoughts, and were not as well armoured. However, they were faster. This allowed them to hunt down and destroy ships less powerful than themselves, and to outrun anything more powerful (such as a dreadnought).

Developed in the late 19th century to be light, fast and manoeuvrable, the first destroyers were designed to counter **torpedo boats**. By the Second World War, their duties were to escort larger craft – both warships and cargo ships – and protect them from enemy surface vessels and submarines. Destroyers are still used today and form the backbone of most modern navies.

The term 'frigate' has been used since the 17th century to describe nimble, **full-rigged** sailing patrol boats. During the Second World War, frigates were metal warships, sized between destroyers and corvettes (see below), tasked with the job of detecting submerged submarines and destroying them with **depth charges**.

Traditionally one of the smallest warship classes during the age of sail, modern corvettes were developed during the Second World War by the British Royal Navy as a swift and manoeuvrable patrol and anti-submarine vessel that could be built quickly and cheaply. Missile-armed corvettes are still used in some modern navies today.

BATTLESHIPS

Developed from the 1860s, the battleship was one of the most important steel warships to enter the world's navies, and underwent constant development as each year passed. These spectacular vessels were designed to search, find, pursue and sink other ships using their many powerful guns. Despite their huge, heavily armoured hulls, they were capable of relatively high speeds and designed to spend many months on the high seas.

Just like their wooden predecessors, the ships of the line (see page 28), battleships bristled with firepower. However, a steel battleship's guns could turn and elevate independently of the ship itself, allowing them to fire in any direction.

Battleships had thick armour plating to protect themselves and their crew from attack. However, the more armour they had, the slower they became, which made them easier to hit, even from afar. As a result, battleships are no longer used today.

Battleships were used extensively during the Second World War. Single, fast battleships were deployed to disrupt trade routes and groups were used to bombard shore defences and protect shipping fleets from air attack. They were rarely able to destroy enemy vessels with their guns, however, and it was clear that the age of the battleship was coming to an end.

The fate of this vessel, the King George V-class battleship HMS *Prince of Wales,* demonstrates how vulnerable the once-mighty battleships were to air attack. Despite its armour and vast number of guns, *Prince of Wales* was sunk by Japanese torpedo bombers in 1941.

AIRCRAFT CARRIERS

Aircraft carriers became vital during the Second World War – especially in the Pacific where vast navies fought for control of the sea. Despite the thousands of big guns these fleets carried, stealthy submarines (see pages 52–53) and aircraft launched from carriers sank the most ships.

Carriers became the most important ships in a fleet. Floating airbases capable of transporting planes anywhere in the world, they used steam-driven catapults to launch the planes off the bow, and metal 'arrestor' wires strung across the flight deck to stop them when they landed.

Carrier-launched aircraft could fly for hundreds of kilometres (far further than any gun-fired shell), seek out enemy ships, attack with bombs or torpedoes, then return to their fleet to re-fuel, re-arm and go again.

This carrier, the USS *Enterprise* (CV-6), was launched in 1936. It had a crew of over 2,000 men, a range of 23,000 km, a top speed of 32.3 knots (60 km/h) and carried around 90 aircraft: fighters, dive-bombers and torpedo-bombers.

SUBMARINES

Unlike other vehicles, the submarine took several centuries of painfully slow development before it became a (relatively) safe and reliable form of transport. This is because submarines have to do many vital and complicated things: they must be watertight; capable of moving forwards, backwards, and up and down in the water; be strong enough to cope with extreme pressure; and carry everything the crew needs to survive while submerged: living spaces, supplies and oxygen.

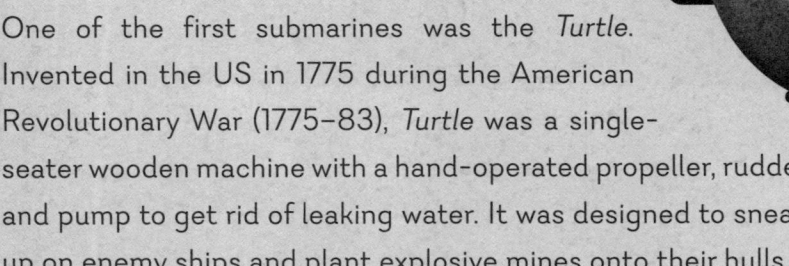

One of the first submarines was the *Turtle*. Invented in the US in 1775 during the American Revolutionary War (1775–83), *Turtle* was a single-seater wooden machine with a hand-operated propeller, rudder and pump to get rid of leaking water. It was designed to sneak up on enemy ships and plant explosive mines onto their hulls.

Launched in 1863 and with a length of 45 metres, French submarine *Plongeur* (meaning 'diver') was exceptionally long for the time. The extra length – needed to house the large compressed-air-powered engine – made the vessel unstable. At the front was a ram, designed to punch holes in the hulls of ships.

Spanish submarine *Ictineo II* (launched 1864) had several revolutionary design features still found on today's submarines. It had two hulls: the inner was watertight; the outer was streamlined, allowing for smooth passage through the water. **Ballast tanks** were flooded to make the submarine sink and pumped with air to make her float.

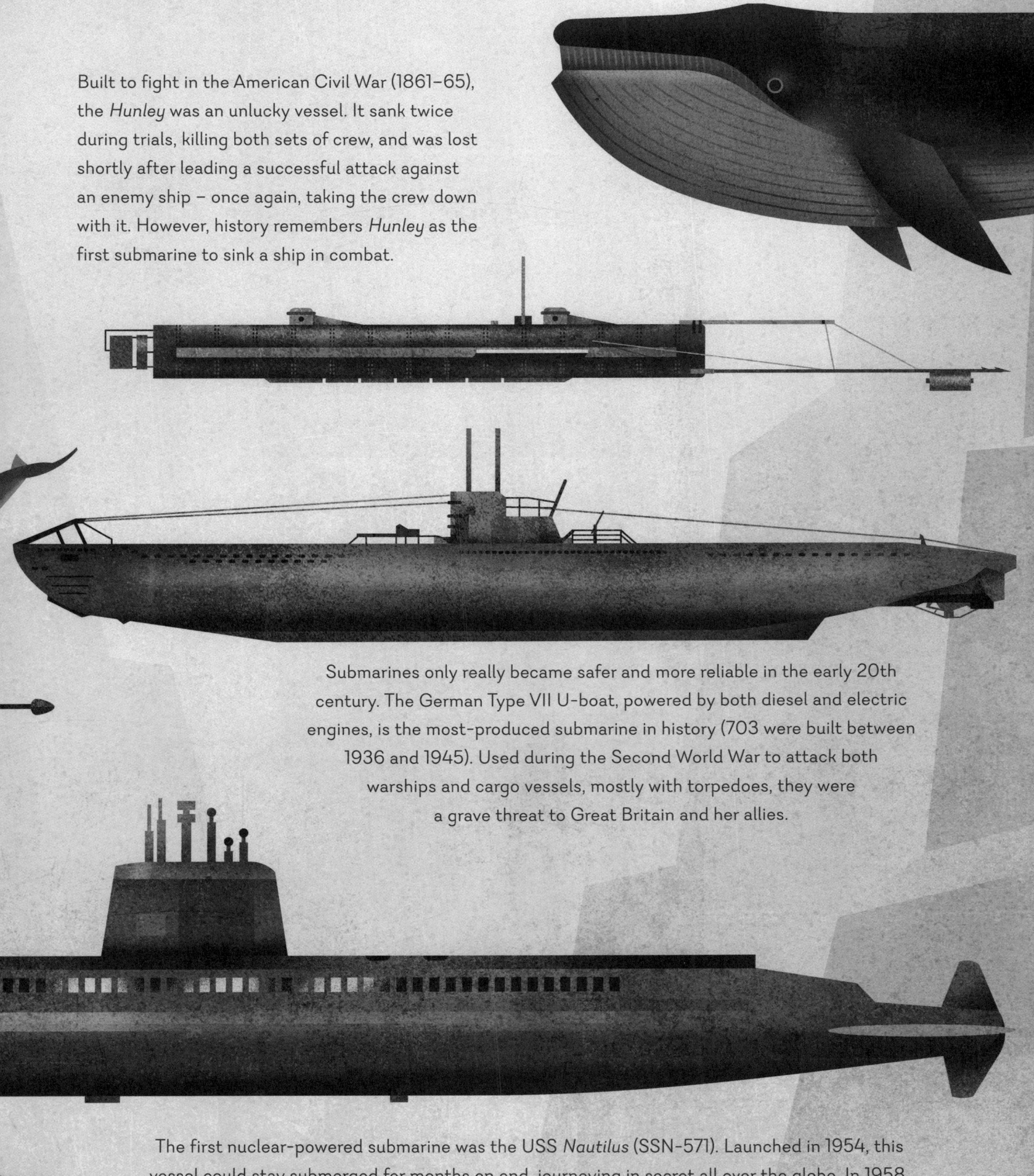

Built to fight in the American Civil War (1861–65), the *Hunley* was an unlucky vessel. It sank twice during trials, killing both sets of crew, and was lost shortly after leading a successful attack against an enemy ship – once again, taking the crew down with it. However, history remembers *Hunley* as the first submarine to sink a ship in combat.

Submarines only really became safer and more reliable in the early 20th century. The German Type VII U-boat, powered by both diesel and electric engines, is the most-produced submarine in history (703 were built between 1936 and 1945). Used during the Second World War to attack both warships and cargo vessels, mostly with torpedoes, they were a grave threat to Great Britain and her allies.

The first nuclear-powered submarine was the USS *Nautilus* (SSN-571). Launched in 1954, this vessel could stay submerged for months on end, journeying in secret all over the globe. In 1958, it even travelled 1,600 km under the ice to reach the North Pole from the United States.

53

– EXTRAORDINARY VESSELS –
TRIESTE

In January 1960, two brave explorers achieved something no one had ever done before. Sitting in a cramped metal sphere hanging beneath the submersible *Trieste*, US naval officer Don Walsh and Swiss engineer Jacques Piccard began an extraordinary – and extraordinarily dangerous – journey to the deepest known part of the ocean: the Challenger Deep in the Pacific. For nearly five hours, the two men listened to their vessel creak and strain as the water pressure outside increased, until they finally reached the lightless depths of the seabed nearly 11 kilometres below the surface.

Trieste's designer, Auguste Piccard (Jacques' father), called it a 'bathyscaphe', which means 'deep ship'. The larger upper portion of the vessel (which looks like a submarine) contained eleven buoyancy tanks. Filled with lighter-than-water petrol, these tanks functioned like the gas bag of a hot air balloon, and meant that *Trieste*

could float. At the start of the journey, *Trieste* was loaded with enough iron pellets to make it slowly and steadily sink. When they had finished exploring the seabed, Piccard and Walsh released the pellets, which lightened the load and allowed the petrol to lift them back to the surface.

The small, cramped gondola beneath the tanks was for the crew; a sphere design was chosen because that is the most pressure-resistant shape. Its walls were made from 13 cm-thick steel and included a single viewing port made from ultra-strong plexiglass. Two propellers, powered by batteries, could push *Trieste* to a speed of around 1 knot (2 km/h). Spotlights illuminated the pitch-black world of the seabed, and proved that life really does exist even at such inhospitable depths.

RESCUE BOATS AND LIFEBOATS

Travelling the seas has never been safer. Boat building safety regulations, ship designs, the materials used to construct them and the technology that keeps them afloat all ensure that most ocean voyages pass without a hitch. But Earth's natural forces are powerful: dangerous weather such as hurricanes and the heavy seas they cause can damage or sink even the largest ships, and accidents such as collisions with other vessels do occur. It's on these rare occasions that rescue boats and lifeboats come into their own.

Off-shore rescue boats (also called all-weather rescue boats) are operated from coastal bases by brave, highly trained crews. These craft are extremely stable and robust, able to cope with heavy seas and dramatic weather even at night or in dense fog. Equipped with powerful searchlights, they can reach a disaster spot quickly and look for lifeboats or people in the sea, rescue them and report their position back to base so other emergency vessels can continue the operation.

Early lifeboats like those found on the RMS *Titanic* (see page 44) were usually wooden rowboats. Capable of carrying around 65 people, each craft would be ideally crewed by a trained sailor or officer who could navigate and keep people calm. Each lifeboat was equipped with an anchor, rope, fresh water, dried food, a compass, lantern, and a mast and sail.

Modern lifeboats (or TEMPSC – Totally Enclosed Motor Propelled Survival Craft) are found on all **merchant ships**, tankers and off-shore oil and gas platforms. These craft have an enclosed living space that keeps the people inside secure, dry and protected from sunstroke and exposure. They have steerable motors, locator beacons, food, water and medical supplies. Their watertight and fireproof hulls are orange so they can be more easily spotted by rescue ships and aircraft.

LEISURE AND RACING BOATS

Not all boats have a job to do or a specific purpose. Some are designed simply for fun and enjoyment – whether it's bobbing on a lake in a rowing boat, whizzing along the shore in a speedboat or venturing into the ocean at the helm of a yacht. Boating can be competitive too, with lots of official races held all over the world every year. Some vessels are specially designed to carry out research both above and below the sea's surface.

Rowing boats are one of the simplest but most widely used boats in history, and their design has not changed much through the centuries. A small, stable craft, they can be propelled by one or more rowers for transport, fishing or simply messing about on the water.

A direct descendent of the Polynesian voyaging canoe (see page 8), catamarans are sail- or engine-propelled vessels with two parallel hulls. This wide design makes them extra stable, even on rough seas. Their sizes range from small single-crew vessels to larger, more ferry-like designs.

Superyachts are large, engine-driven boats with an emphasis on luxury and comfort. Due to their size, they usually have a dedicated crew. Some are large enough to have swimming pools, jet skis, bars and several decks for passengers to relax on.

Speedboats are small leisure craft propelled by powerful petrol engines. These engines can be built into the boat's structure (inboard motors) or attached to the back (outboard motors). Speedboats, as the name suggests, are designed to zoom across the water quickly.

BOATS TIMELINE

Of all the forms of transport devised by humans, boats have had the longest time to advance and develop. The first were powered by the pilot's muscles – either by using their hands, or paddles and oars. The invention of the sail allowed the wind to be harnessed, and much later came the use of engines. Who knows what further advances will occur in the world of watercraft?

8040–7510 BCE
The Pesse canoe, the oldest known boat in existence, is carved by hunter-gatherers in what is now the Netherlands.

AROUND 1500 BCE
Southeast Asian explorers begin to venture across the Pacific in Polynesian canoes.

FROM 900 BCE
Ancient Phoenician traders are the first people to navigate the Mediterranean Sea.

1906
Launch of HMS *Dreadnought*, one of the most influential steel battleships.

1886–96
The clipper *Cutty Sark* holds the record for the fastest sea voyage from Australia to England.

1838
SS *Archimedes*, the first ship to be successfully powered by steam, is launched.

1912
RMS *Titanic* collides with an iceberg, sinking with the loss of more than 1,500 lives.

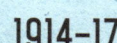

1914–17
Ernest Shackleton leads the Imperial Trans-Antarctic Expedition, but fails to complete the first land crossing of the Antarctic via the South Pole.

1950s
The first purpose-built container ships are constructed.

800–1200 CE
Viking dragonships rule the seas of northern Europe.

AROUND 1000 CE
Leif Erikson sails across the Atlantic, becoming probably the first European visitor to North America.

1519–22
Spanish navigator Juan Sebastián Elcano completes the first round-the-world voyage by sea.

2ND CENTURY CE
The first junks are invented in China.

1765
The launch of HMS *Victory*, one of the most powerful warships of its era.

16TH–19TH CENTURIES
Around 12 million Africans are forced into slavery, crossing the Atlantic on specially built slave ships.

1650–1730
During the Golden Age of Piracy, pirates rule the waters of the Atlantic, Caribbean Sea and Indian Ocean, plundering trade.

15TH–17TH CENTURIES
The Age of Exploration – European explorers sail across the globe on missions of discovery, trade and conquest.

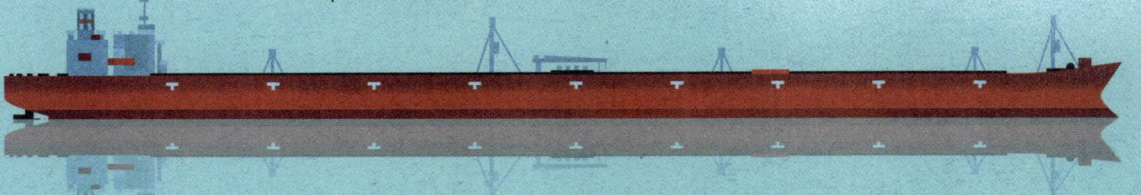

1960
The submersible *Trieste* descends to Challenger Deep in the Pacific, the deepest known part of the ocean.

1977
Spirit of Australia sets the world water speed record of 511.11 km/h.

1979
Seawise Giant, the largest ship ever built, is launched.

2022
Maiden voyage of *Icon of the Seas*, the world's largest cruise ship.

RECORD BREAKERS

Maritime technology has had far longer to develop – many thousands of years, in fact – than any other form of transportation, and the unique properties of water mean that ships can be far larger and heavier than land or airborne vehicles. Here are some of the most amazing waterborne world records.

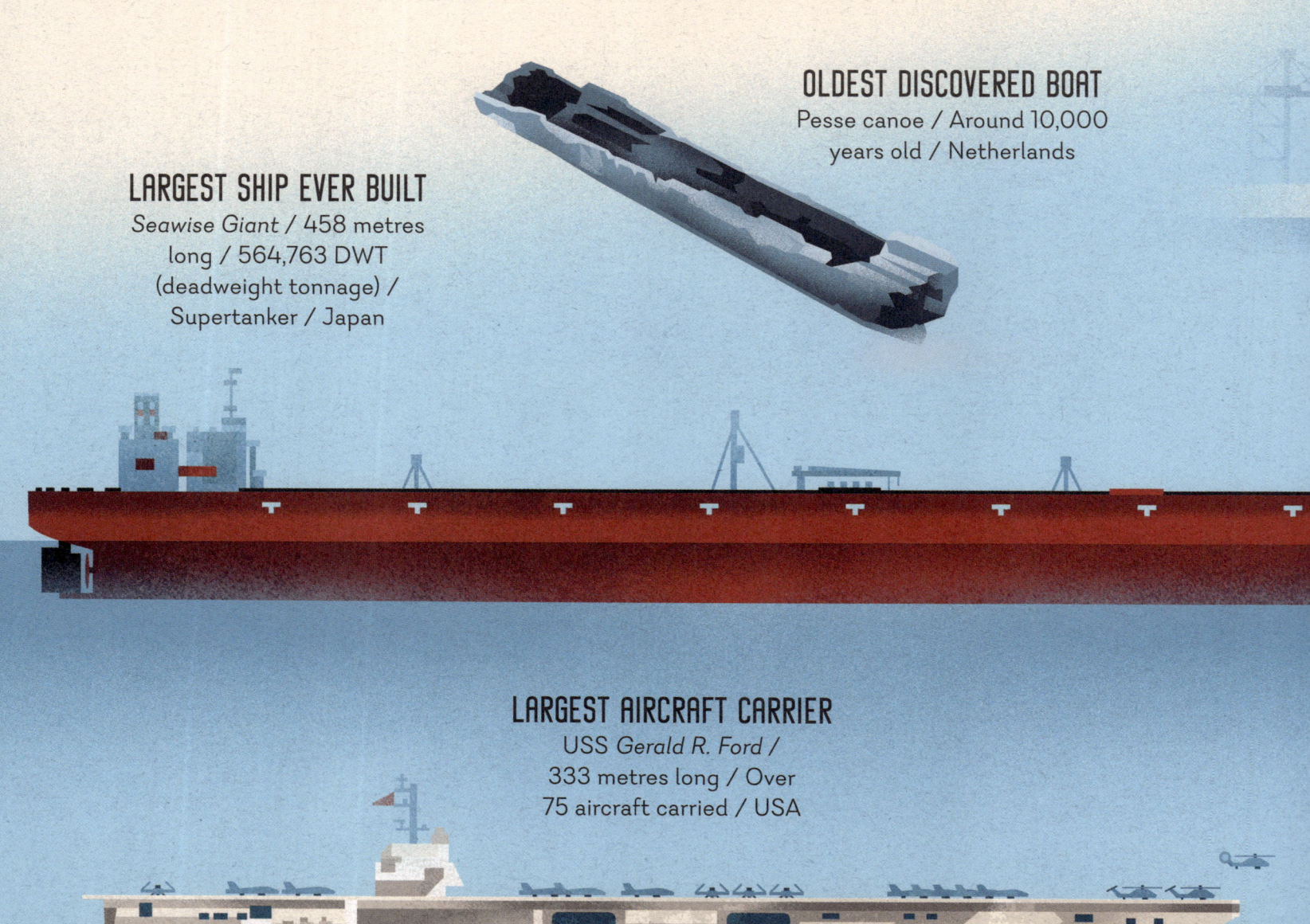

OLDEST DISCOVERED BOAT
Pesse canoe / Around 10,000 years old / Netherlands

LARGEST SHIP EVER BUILT
Seawise Giant / 458 metres long / 564,763 DWT (deadweight tonnage) / Supertanker / Japan

LARGEST AIRCRAFT CARRIER
USS *Gerald R. Ford* / 333 metres long / Over 75 aircraft carried / USA

DEEPEST KNOWN SHIPWRECK
USS *Samuel B. Roberts* / 6,895 metres / Destroyer / Sunk 1944 in the Philippine Sea

GLOSSARY

ADMIRAL
Commander of a fleet or navy – the most senior naval rank.

ANTI-BOARDING NETTING
Netting stretched above the deck of a ship to prevent enemy sailors from getting onboard.

ARMADA
A fleet of warships. The Spanish Armada is the name of a specific invading fleet launched in 1588 against England.

AUTOPILOT
Automatic pilot; a device that controls and steers a vehicle without the need for human involvement.

BALLAST TANK
A device used on submarines and lighter-than-air vehicles (such as hot air balloons) to control the rate of ascent and descent.

BARQUENTINE
A type of three-masted sailing vessel.

BOW
The front of a boat or ship (the rear is called the stern).

CAPITAL SHIP
A general term describing any kind of large warship, such as an aircraft carrier or battleship.

CASEMATE
An armoured enclosure for guns on a warship (named after small rooms in castles from where archers shot arrows).

DEPTH CHARGE
An anti-submarine explosive device designed to detonate at a particular depth underwater.

FULL-RIGGED
A full-rigged ship is a sailing vessel with three or more masts with rigged sails on each.

GPS
Global Positioning System: a service that conveys accurate locational and geographical information on electronic devices such as computers, smartphones and tablets.

HUNTER-GATHERER
An often-nomadic culture of people who find food by foraging for vegetation, hunting for animals and fishing.

KNOT
Nautical mile per hour: a measurement of speed equivalent to 1.85 km/h (1 nautical mile = 1.85 km).

LATEEN SAIL
A sail shaped like a triangle.

LIST
When a ship leans either to port or starboard; if the list gets too bad it can lead to the vessel capsizing.

MARAUD
The act of roaming an area on the hunt for people to rob and plunder.

MERCANTILE
Relating to the act of trade or commerce; a mercantile vessel carries goods.

MERCHANT SHIP
A ship used for trade, rather than for military purposes or transporting passengers.

MESOLITHIC
A period during the Stone Age, occurring between the Palaeolithic and Neolithic.

MUTINY
An act of open rebellion by sailors or soldiers against their commanding officers. Mutiny was a crime with harsh punishments.

PENNANT
A type of flag that tapers to a point (making it triangle shaped), used for signal communications between vessels.

PORT
The left-hand side of a boat or ship.

PROW
The front of a vessel (also called the bow).

SEA TRIAL
A voyage to test the seaworthiness of a newly launched vessel.

SLOOP
A type of small, single-masted sailing ship.

SQUARE SAIL
A sail in the shape of a square.

STARBOARD
The right-hand side of a boat or ship.

STEAM TURBINE
A type of engine that converts the heat energy from steam to be used in mechanical work, such as turning the propeller on a ship.

SWIVEL GUN
A small cannon fitted to the side of ships that can be moved (swivelled) by the user to aim at enemy crew.

TORPEDO BOAT
A small, fast motorboat used to launch torpedoes at enemy ships.

TUG
A small, powerful and nimble vessel often used to manoeuvre large vessels (such as container ships) around ports, harbours and docks.

WEATHER DECK
A deck without a roof that is open to the weather.

INDEX

A
admirals 28, 62
Age of Exploration 16–19
aircraft 50–51
aircraft carriers 50–51, 60–61
American Civil War 38–39, 53
Antarctic 40–41, 58
anti-boarding netting 15, 62
Archimedes, SS 36, 58
armour plating 49
autopilots 43, 62

B
ballast tanks 52, 62
barquentines 40, 62
bathyscaphe 54–55
battlecruisers 46–47
battles 28–29
battleships 46–49, 58
Bellamy, Samuel 34–35
'Black Bart' 33
'Blackbeard' 32, 33
Blackwall frigate 20
block construction 24
boatswains 31
Bonny, Anne 33
bottom trawling 43
Britannia, RMS 36
British Royal Navy 30
broadsides 28
Brunel, Isambard Kingdom 36, 37
bulk carriers 42
buoyancy tanks 54–55
Byzantine empire 13

C
'Calico Jack' 33
cannons 28, 29
canoes 8, 58, 60
capital ships 47, 62
caravels 13
cargo ships 42
carpenters 29, 31
carracks 14, 16, 18, 28
casemates 39, 62
catamarans 57
Challenger Deep 54–55
Charles I, King of Spain 18–19
China 12, 59
clippers 20, 22, 58
cogs 13
combustion engine 6
Concepción 18
container ports 26–27
container ships 26–27, 42, 58
corvettes 48
cranes 25
cruise ships 59, 61
Cutty Sark 22–23, 58
Cyclops, HMS 37

D
depth charges 48, 62
destroyers 48
dragonships 10–11, 59
Dreadnought, HMS 46–47, 58
dreadnoughts 47
dry docks 25
dugout boats 6, 8

E
East Indiamen 20
Elcano, Juan Sebastián 19, 59
Endurance 40–41
enslavement 17, 20, 21
Enterprise, USS 50–51
Erikson, Leif 11, 59
exploration 16–19, 59

F
Fiery Cross 22
first-rate ships 28
fishing boats 43
Francis I, King of France 14
frigates 20, 48

G
galleons 28, 32
galleys 9, 13
gauloi 9
Gerald R. Ford, USS 60
Golden Age of Sail 20–21
GPS navigation 43, 62
Great Britain, SS 36
Great Eastern, SS 37
Greeks, ancient 9

H
Harland & Wolff 37, 44
Henry VIII 14–15
Hornigold, Benjamin 33
Hunley 53
hunter-gatherers 8, 62

I J K
icebergs 45
Icon of the Seas 59, 61
Ictineo II 52
Imperial Trans-Antarctic Expedition 40–41, 58
indigenous peoples 17, 20
ironclads 38–39, 46
junks 12, 59
knarrs 12

L
largest ships 60–61
lateen sails 13
Liberty ship 61
lifeboats 56
listing 62

M
Magellan, Ferdinand 18–19
marines 29, 31
Mary Rose 14–15
medieval period 12–13
merchant ships 20, 56, 63
Merrimack 39
midshipmen 30
Missouri, USS 37
Monitor, USS 38–39
muskets 29
mutiny 63

N
Nautilus, USS 53
navies 28–29
Nelson, Horatio 30
New Providence, Bahamas 32
nuclear power 53
Oceanic, SS 37
oldest boat 8, 58, 60
Ottoman empire 13

P Q
paddlewheels 37
pennants 14, 63
pentecontors 9
Persians, ancient 9
Pesse canoe 8, 58, 60
Phoenicians, ancient 9, 58
Piccard, Auguste 54–55
Piccard, Jacques 54–55
Pirate Republic 32, 33
pirates 13, 20, 32–33, 34–35, 59
Plongeur 52
Polynesians 8, 58
ports 26–27, 61
Prince of Wales, HMS 49
propellers 36
Queen Anne's Revenge 32

R
Rackham, John 'Calico Jack' 33
rafts 6
ram (weapon) 9, 52
Ranger 33
Rattler, HMS 37
Read, Mary 33
rescue boats 56
Roberts, Bartholomew 'Black Bart' 33
Romans, ancient 9
round ships 9
rowing 9, 11
rowing boats 57
Royal Mail Ships (RMS) 36

S
sail types 13, 62, 63
sailor ranks 31
Samuel B. Roberts, USS 60
San Antonio 18, 19
Santiago 18
screw propellers 36
sea trials 63
Seawise Giant 42, 59, 60–61
second-rate ships 28
Second World War 48–51, 53
Seringapatam 20
Shackleton, Ernest 40–41, 58

Shanghai seaport 61
ships of the line 28–29
shipwrecks 35, 45, 60
shipyards 24–25
slave trade 21, 59
sloops 34, 35, 63
speed records 23, 59, 61
speedboats 57
spices 16, 18
Spirit of Australia 59, 61
steam ships 36–37, 58
steam turbines 47, 63
steel ships 46–47
Strait of Magellan 19
submarines 52–53
submersibles 54–55, 59
supertankers 42
superyachts 57
surgeons 29

T
tankers 42, 56
tea clippers 20
Teach, Edward 'Blackbeard' 32, 33
TEMPSC (Totally Enclosed Motor Propelled Survival Craft) 56
third-rate ships 28
Titanic, RMS 37, 44–45, 56, 58
torpedo boats 48, 63
trade 16, 18, 20–21, 26–27
trawlers 43
tree trunk boats 6, 8
Trieste 54–55, 59
Trinidad 18, 19
triremes 9
tugs 41, 63
Turtle 52

U V
U-boats 53
'ultra large crude carriers' (ULCC) 42
Venetian republic 13
Victoria 18, 19
Victory, HMS 30–31, 59
Vikings 11, 12, 59
Virginia, CSS 38–39

W Y
Walsh, Don 54–55
warrant officers 31
warships 14, 28–29, 38–39, 46–47
weather decks 15, 63
White Star Line 37, 44
Whydah Gally 34–35
yachts 57
Yelcho 41

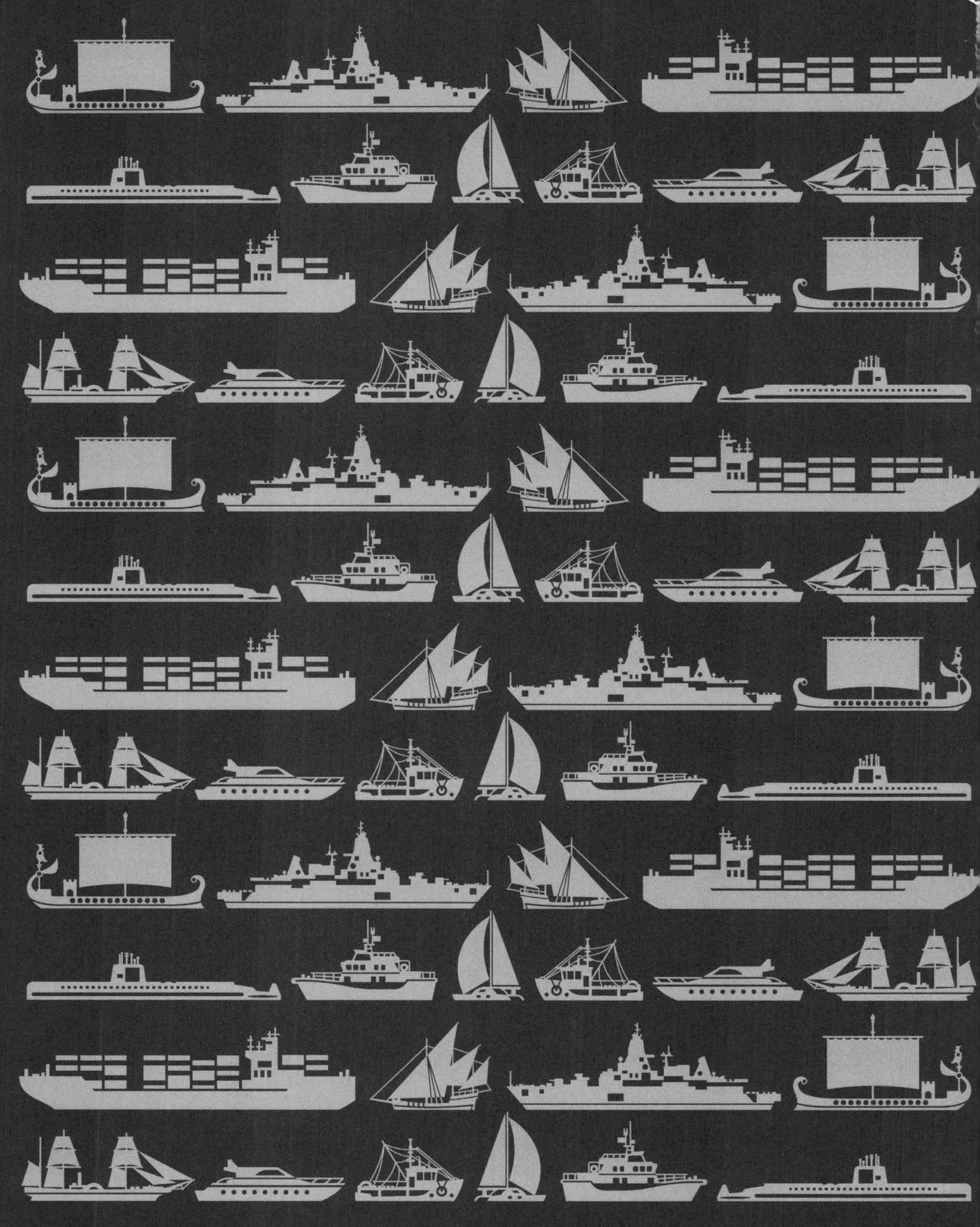